Editor
Gisela Lee

Editorial Manager
Karen J. Goldfluss, M.S. Ed.

Editor in Chief
Sharon Coan, M.S. Ed.

Illustrator
Victoria Ponikvar-Frazier

Cover Artist
Jessica Orlando

Art Coordinator
Denice Adorno

Creative Director
Elayne Roberts

Imaging
James Edward Grace

Product Manager
Phil Garcia

Publisher
Mary D. Smith, M.S. Ed.

How to Multiply

Grades 2–3

Author

Mary Rosenberg

Teacher Created Resources, Inc.
6421 Industry Way
Westminster, CA 92683
www.teachercreated.com

ISBN: 978-1-57690-945-4

©2000 Teacher Created Resources, Inc.
Reprinted, 2014
Made in U.S.A.

Table of Contents

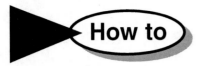

A Note to Teachers and Parents

Welcome to the "How to" math series! You have chosen one of over two dozen books designed to give your children the information and practice they need to acquire important concepts in specific areas of math. The goal of the "How to" math books is to give children an extra boost as they work toward mastery of the math skills established by the National Council of Teachers of Mathematics (NCTM) and outlined in grade-level scope and sequence guidelines. The NCTM standards encourage children to learn basic math concepts and skills and apply them to new situations and real-world events. The children learn to justify their solutions through the use of pictures, numbers, words, graphs, and diagrams.

The design of this book is intended to allow it to be used by teachers or parents for a variety of purposes and needs. Each of the units contains one or more "How to" pages and two or more practice pages. The "How to" section of each unit precedes the practice pages and provides needed information such as a concept or math rule review, important terms and formulas to remember, or step-by-step guidelines necessary for using the practice pages. While most "How to" pages are written for direct use by the children, in some lower-grade level books these pages are presented as instructional pages or direct lessons to be used by a teacher or parent prior to introducing the practice pages. In this book, the "How to" pages detail the concepts that will be covered in the pages that follow as well as how to teach the concept(s). Many of the "How to" pages also include "Learning Notes" and "Teaching the Lesson." Each unit is sequential and builds upon the ideas covered in the previous unit(s).

About This Book

Each unit begins with a "How to" page which includes "Learning Notes." The "Learning Notes" tell what concepts will be covered in the following practice pages as well as ideas on how to present the concepts to the children. The practice pages review and introduce new skills and provide opportunities for the children to use the newly acquired skills in new situations. When working with multiplication, it is important to give the children many concrete experiences in learning the basic multiplication facts. These experiences can be created through the use of basic manipulatives, such as multilink cubes, beans, buttons, pennies, etc. The more experiences the children have with manipulatives, the easier it will be for them to learn the basic facts and apply the skills to other multiplication experiences. Each unit is sequential and builds upon the ideas and skills covered in previous units.

The activities in this book will help children learn new skills or reinforce skills already learned in the following areas:

- multiplying 2-, 3-, and 4-digit numbers with and without regrouping
- multiplying numbers with decimals
- estimating products
- rounding numbers to the nearest hundred
- using a graph for information
- solving word problems
- finding the volume
- addition and subtraction skills
- skip counting

- writing multiplication problems both vertically and horizontally
- order of operation
- vocabulary of multiplication
- finding the missing product or factor
- using symbols ($<$, $>$, $=$) to compare numbers
- finding patterns in numbers
- visiting a Web site to practice multiplication skills

The units in this book are designed to match the suggestions of the National Council of Teachers of Mathematics (NCTM). They strongly support the learning of addition and subtraction and other processes in the context of problem solving and real-world applications. Use every opportunity to have students apply these new skills in classroom situations and at home. This will reinforce the value of the skill as well as the process. The activities in this book match the following NCTM standards:

Problem Solving

The children develop and apply strategies to solve problems, verify and interpret results, sort and classify objects, and solve word problems.

Communication

The children are able to communicate mathematical solutions through manipulatives, pictures, diagrams, numbers, and words. Children are able to relate everyday language to the language and symbols of math. Children have opportunities to read, write, discuss, and listen to math ideas.

Reasoning

Children make logical conclusions through interpreting graphs, patterns, and facts. The children are able to explain and justify their math problems.

Connections

Children are able to apply math concepts and skills to other curricular areas and to the real world.

Estimation

Children explore estimation strategies and develop the skill to determine when it is appropriate to use an estimate and whether an estimate is reasonable for the given situation.

Number Sense and Numeration

Children learn to count, label, and sort collections as well as learn the basic math operations.

Concepts of Whole Number Operations

Children develop an understanding for the operation (addition, subtraction) by modeling and discussing situations, and relating math language and the symbols of operation ($+, -, \times, \div$) to the problem being discussed.

Whole Number Computation

Children are able to model, explain, and develop competency in basic facts, mental computation, and estimation techniques.

Geometry and Spatial Sense

Children are able to describe, model, draw and classify shapes, and relate geometric ideas to number and measurement ideas.

Measurement

Children use measurement (time, distance, weight, volume, area, etc.) and estimates of measurement in problem solving and in everyday situations.

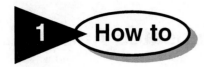

Learning Notes

In this unit children will . . .

- learn that multiplication is the same as "repeated addition."
- develop the concept of multiplication by using pictures.
- practice skip counting and relate this skill to learning the multiplication facts.
- write the multiplication problem for a given set of pictures.
- learn the vocabulary of multiplication—factors, products, etc.

Materials

- 3" x 5" (8 cm x 13 cm) index cards
- small stickers or small stamps

Teaching the Lesson

1. Before completing the practice sheets, introduce the concept of multiplication through the use of concrete materials. Using the index cards, stickers, and stamps, make various sets of picture cards. (See the example below.)

2. Show the children the three index cards with the pictures on them. Ask the children to write/tell how many moose there are in mathematical terms. The children might say 3 + 3 + 3 = 9. Show the children a "faster way" to write the problem. Ask the children, "How many cards are there?" (3 cards) Ask the children, "How many moose heads are on each card?" (3 heads)

3. Model how to write the multiplication problem.

3 ☐ **x 3**  **= 9**

(cards)　　　(moose heads on each card)　　　(moose heads in all)

4. Go over different sets of index cards with the children and take the children through the same steps outlined above.

5. Give each child a set of index cards and some stamps or stickers to create a set of multiplication cards.

6. Go over the practice sheets with the children. Model how to solve each problem.

Multiplication is the same as adding the same number over and over.

Count and add the triangles (2 + 2 = 4).

You can also multiply 2 twos (or 2 x 2) and get the same result or product (4).

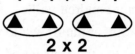

$$1 + 1 + 1 + 1$$
$$2 \times 2$$

Directions: Circle groups of two. How many sets of two were made? What is the product (answer)?

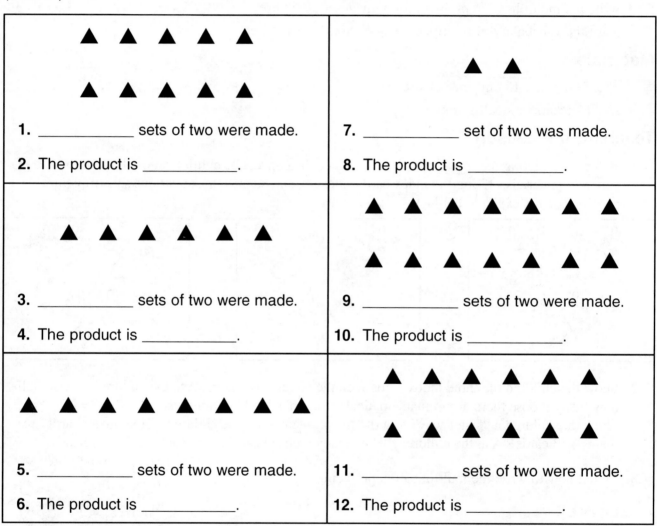

1. _____ sets of two were made.

2. The product is _____.

7. _____ set of two was made.

8. The product is _____.

3. _____ sets of two were made.

4. The product is _____.

9. _____ sets of two were made.

10. The product is _____.

5. _____ sets of two were made.

6. The product is _____.

11. _____ sets of two were made.

12. The product is _____.

Directions: Skip counting can help make it easier to learn multiplication facts. Finish the skip counting pattern for each row.

13. 0, 2, 4, _____, _____, _____, _____, _____, _____, _____, _____, _____, _____

14. 0, 4, 8, _____, _____, _____, _____, _____, _____, _____, _____, _____, _____

15. 0, 5, 10, _____, _____, _____, _____, _____, _____, _____, _____, _____, _____

16. 0, 6, 12, _____, _____, _____, _____, _____, _____, _____, _____, _____, _____

Multiplication is a faster way to add sets with the same number of items.

Count and add the stars below (3 + 3 + 3 = 9).

You can get the same number of stars by multiplying the number of sets times the number of items in each set (3 sets of stars x 3 stars in each set = 9 stars).

3 stars + 3 stars + 3 stars = 9 stars

3 sets of stars x 3 items in each set = 9 stars

Directions: Count the number of sets and items in each set. Write the addition problem and the multiplication problem for each set of pictures.

1. _____ + _____ + _____ + _____ = _____   **3.** _____ + _____ = _____

2. _____ x _____ = _____   **4.** _____ x _____ = _____
    (sets)   (items)   (product)   (sets)   (items)   (product)

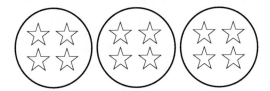   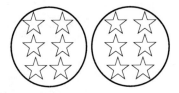

5. _____ + _____ + _____ = _____   **7.** _____ + _____ = _____

6. _____ x _____ = _____   **8.** _____ x _____ = _____
    (sets)   (items)   (product)   (sets)   (items)   (product)

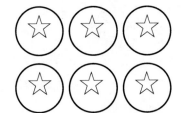   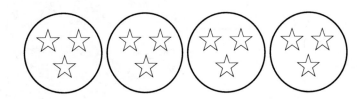

9. ___ + ___ + ___ + ___ + ___ + ___ = ___   **11.** _____ + _____ + _____ + _____ = _____

10. _____ x _____ = _____   **12.** _____ x _____ = _____
    (sets)   (items)   (product)   (sets)   (items)   (product)

In multiplication, the two numbers being multiplied are called "factors." The answer is called the "product."

  x

| 2 sets of umbrellas | x | 2 umbrellas in each set | = | 4 |
| (factor) | | (factor) | | (product) |

Directions: Look at each set of problems. Circle the sets. Then write the product (answer) for the 2 factors.

1. 3 x 2 = _____

2. 5 x 2 = _____

3. 1 x 2 = _____

4. 2 x 2 = _____

5. 4 x 2 = _____

6. 7 x 2 = _____

7. 6 x 2 = _____

8. 2 x 9 = _____

Learning Notes

In this unit children will . . .

- complete a chart on the multiplication facts for numbers multiplied by 2.
- draw sets of pictures and solve the multiplication problem.
- learn to multiply by 2's and 3's.
- learn the commutative property of multiplication.
- read a word problem and write the appropriate multiplication factors and product.
- write the missing factor or product.

Materials

- small manipulatives—multilink cubes, beans, pennies, etc.
- paper with 10 circles drawn on it
- math journals or a piece of paper

Teaching the Lesson

1. Review the concept of multiplication using the small manipulatives and the paper with the circles drawn on it.
2. Ask the children to show 2 circles with 5 pennies in each circle.

What is the multiplication problem?

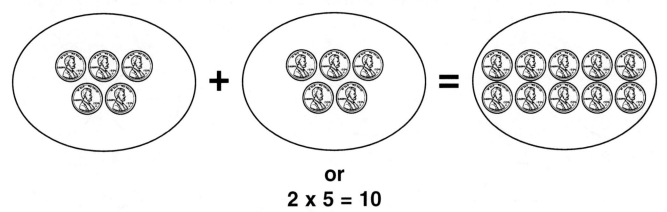

or
2 x 5 = 10

What is the product (answer)? 10

3. Have the children draw a picture of the multiplication problem as well as record the multiplication problem in their math journals or on a piece of paper.
4. Give the children many opportunities to model and solve different multiplication problems.
5. Go over the work sheets with the children.

Note: Children who are not sure of the basic multiplication process should continue to use manipulatives and circles to model and solve the multiplication problems. As the children become more comfortable and confident in their multiplication skills, they will become less reliant on using manipulatives in solving multiplication problems.

Doubling the digit (number) when adding is the same as multiplying the digit by 2.

 **+**  **is the same as**  **X**

3 **+** **3 = 6**   **2 (sets) x 3 (items in each set) = 6**

Directions: Complete the chart below by multiplying each number in the top row by 2.

x	1	2	3	4	5	6	7	8	9	10
2										

Directions: Draw sets of dots to show each multiplication problem. Solve each problem and write the answer on the line.

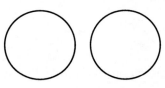

1. 2 x 1 = _____

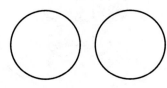

4. 2 x 7 = _____

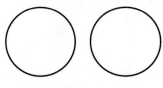

7. 2 x 2 = _____

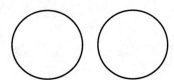

2. 2 x 9 = _____

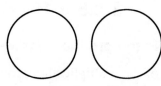

5. 2 x 4 = _____

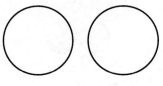

8. 2 x 0 = _____

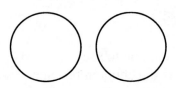

3. 2 x 6 = _____

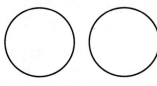

6. 2 x 10 = _____

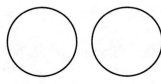

9. 2 x 3 = _____

When multiplying two numbers, the order of the factors does not change the product (answer).

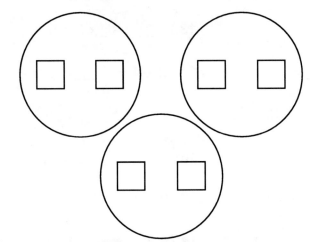

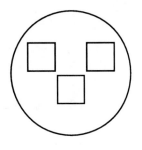

3 sets of 2 items

2 sets of 3 items

3 x 2 = 6

2 x 3 = 6

Directions: Count by 3's to complete the pattern.

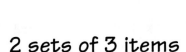

0, 3, _____, _____, _____, _____, _____, 21, _____, _____, _____

Directions: Use the pattern above to solve each multiplication problem. Draw a line matching the two multiplication problems with the same answer. The first one has been done for you.

1. 3 x 1 = __3__

2. 3 x 9 = _____

3. 3 x 7 = _____

4. 3 x 4 = _____

5. 3 x 10 = _____

6. 3 x 5 = _____

7. 3 x 8 = _____

8. 3 x 3 = _____

9. 3 x 6 = _____

A. 9 x 3 = _____

B. 5 x 3 = _____

C. 6 x 3 = _____

D. 7 x 3 = _____

E. 4 x 3 = _____

F. 3 x 3 = _____

G. 1 x 3 = __3__

H. 8 x 3 = _____

I. 10 x 3 = _____

Directions: Complete each table by writing the missing factor or product.

1. 2 x 1 = _____

2. 2 x _____ = 2

3. _____ x 3 = 6

4. 2 x _____ = 8

5. 2 x 5 = _____

6. _____ x 6 = 12

7. 2 x 7 = _____

8. 2 x _____ = 16

9. _____ x 9 = 18

10. 2 x 10 = _____

11. 3 x _____ = 3

12. 3 x 2 = _____

13. _____ x 3 = 9

14. 3 x 4 = _____

15. 3 x _____ = 15

16. _____ x 6 = 18

17. 3 x 7 = _____

18. 3 x _____ = 24

Directions: Answer each word problem and write the multiplication problem.

19. Joanie has 2 marble bags. Inside each bag, there are 6 marbles. How many marbles does Joanie have in all? Joanie has _____ marbles in all.	22. Mary has 3 dogs. Each dog can eat 5 dog biscuits a day. How many dog biscuits do Mary's dogs eat in a day? Mary's dogs eat _____ dog biscuits a day.
20. Each basket holds 2 apples. How many apples will the 8 baskets hold in all? The 8 baskets will hold _____ apples in all.	23. Katie has 3 books. If she reads 10 pages in each book every day, how many pages does Katie read in a day? Katie reads _____ pages a day.
21. Frances has 3 spiders. Each spider laid 9 eggs. How many spider eggs are there in all? There are _____ spider eggs in all.	24. Sasha is having a birthday party. She invited 15 friends to the party. If each friend gets 2 cupcakes, how many cupcakes does Sasha need to buy? Sasha needs to buy _____ cupcakes.

Learning Notes

In this unit children will . . .

- learn the rule for multiplying by 0 and 1.
- learn that a multiplication problem can be written horizontally or vertically without changing the product.
- learn to multiply by 4's and 5's.

Materials

- small manipulatives—buttons, pennies, beans, multilink cubes, etc.
- paper with 10 circles drawn on it

Teaching the Lesson

1. Use the circles and small manipulatives to model how to multiply by 0. Discuss the rule that when multiplying a factor by 0 the answer is always 0. Have the children "fill" 2 of the circles with 0 manipulatives. What is the total number of manipulatives? 0

   What is the multiplication problem? 2 x 0 = 0

2. Have the children model 2 x 0 = 0 x 2 (commutative property of multiplication). Take 2 circles and "fill" with no manipulatives. What is the answer? 0

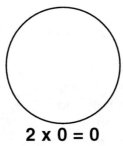 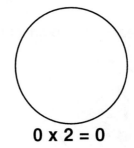

2 x 0 = 0   **0 x 2 = 0**

3. Complete the top half of the multiplying by 0's and 1's practice sheet (page 14).

4. Again, using the manipulatives and the circles, introduce multiplying by 1. Discuss the rule that when multiplying by 1, the product is always the same as the other factor.

 x 1 **is the same as**

5. Have the children use one circle and place three items in the circle. What is the math problem? 1 (circle) x 3 (items) = 3

6. Have the children use the idea of commutative property and model 3 (circles) x 1 (item in each circle) = 3.

7. Have the children complete the bottom half of the multiplying by 0's and 1's practice sheet (page 14).

8. For the multiplying by 4's and multiplying by 5's practice sheets (pages 15 and 16), model how to solve the problems with the children.

Multiplying by 0 is easy. The product is always 0! Look at the examples.

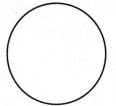 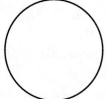 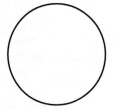 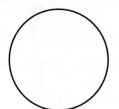 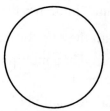

3 sets x 0 in each set = 0   **2 sets x 0 in each set = 0**

3 x 0 = 0   **2 x 0 = 0**

Directions: Write the product to each problem on the line.

1. 10 x 0 = _____   **5.** 0 x 3 = _____   **9.** 3 x 0 = _____

2. 8 x 0 = _____   **6.** 0 x 9 = _____   **10.** 1 x 0 = _____

3. 0 x 0 = _____   **7.** 2 x 0 = _____   **11.** 6 x 0 = _____

4. 5 x 0 = _____   **8.** 4 x 0 = _____   **12.** 0 x 7 = _____

Multiplying by 1's is also easy. The product is always the same as the other factor.

There is one set with one butterfly in each set, and 1 is the other factor so the product is 1.    There are 2 sets with 1 bear in each set, and 2 is the other factor so the product is 2.

1 x 1 = 1   **2 x 1 = 2**

Directions: Write the product to each problem on the line.

13. 1 x 3 = _____   **17.** 1 x 5 = _____   **21.** 1 x 8 = _____

14. 9 x 1 = _____   **18.** 4 x 1 = _____   **22.** 1 x 4 = _____

15. 3 x 1 = _____   **19.** 10 x 1 = _____   **23.** 2 x 1 = _____

16. 8 x 1 = _____   **20.** 1 x 9 = _____   **24.** 1 x 10 = _____

Multiplication problems can also be written vertically.

4	x	5	=	20	**is the same as**	4	factor
factor		factor		product		x 5	factor
						20	product

Directions: Rewrite each multiplication problem vertically. Solve each problem.

1.

4 x 3 =

x

2.

4 x 7 =

x

3.

4 x 9 =

x

4.

4 x 4 =

x

5.

4 x 2 =

x

6.

4 x 8 =

x

Directions: Solve each multiplication problem. Write the letter that goes with the answer for each problem on the line at the bottom of the page.

5	10	15	20	25	30	35	40	45	50	55
A	C	I	L	M	N	O	P	T	U	Y

1.

    2
  x 5
  ☐

2.

    5
  x 1
  ☐

3.

    6
  x 5
  ☐

4.

    5
  x 11
  ☐

5.

    5
  x 7
  ☐

6.

   10
  x 5
  ☐

7.

    5
  x 5
  ☐

8.

    5
  x 10
  ☐

9.

    5
  x 4
  ☐

10.

    5
  x 9
  ☐

11.

    3
  x 5
  ☐

12.

    8
  x 5
  ☐

13.

    4
  x 5
  ☐

14.

   11
  x 5
  ☐

___ ___ ___   ___ ___ ___   ___ ___ ___ ___ ___ ___ ___ ___?
 1   2   3   4   5   6   7   8   9 10 11 12 13 14

Learning Notes

In this unit children will . . .

- learn to multiply by 6's, 7's, and 8's.
- compare two numbers using the < (less than), > (greater than), or = (equal to) symbols.
- fill in the missing factor or product.
- discover the pattern that is made when counting by 7's.

Materials

- playing cards of one deck with the face cards removed or six 3" x 5" (8 cm x 13 cm) index cards cut in half (3" x 2 ½" or 8 cm x 7 cm) and numbered 0–10
- crayons or markers
- small manipulatives (buttons, multilink cubes, beans, etc.) and paper with circles drawn on it for children who are having difficulty in mastering basic multiplication facts

Teaching the Lesson

1. Before introducing the practice sheets, "warm up" the children by skip counting by 6's, 7's, and 8's to 100 (or more).

2. Record the numbers on the chalkboard or on a large piece of butcher paper. For each number, have the children generate the multiplication problem. Record the problems on the chalkboard or on the butcher paper. The children can use this information (if needed) when completing the work sheets.

30	36	42	48	54	60
6 x 5 = 30	6 x 6 = 36	6 x 7 = 42	6 x 8 = 48	6 x 9 = 54	6 x 10 = 60

3. Go over the practice sheets with the children.

Extension

Have the children remove the face cards from a deck of playing cards. Shuffle the cards and place in a stack facedown. Turn over the top two cards and create two multiplication problems (fact families). Record the problems in a math journal or on a piece of paper. Continue making multiplication problems until all of the playing cards have been used.

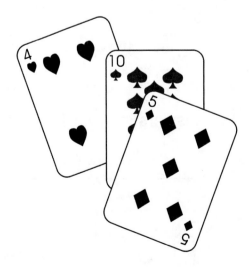

Card Shuffle

Directions: Remove from a deck of playing cards the ace, 2, 3, 4, 5, 6, 7, 8, 9, and 10 cards of one suit. Shuffle these cards and place in a stack facedown. Turn over the top card. Write the number in the box. Multiply the 6 by the number you wrote in the box and write the answer.

Step 1:
Turn over the top card.

Step 2:
Write the number in the box.

$$\begin{array}{r} 6 \\ \times\ \boxed{10} \\ \hline \end{array}$$

Step 3: Multiply the 6 by the 10. Write the product (answer) below the line. Repeat the steps until all of the cards have been used.

$$\begin{array}{r} 6 \\ \times\ \boxed{10} \\ \hline 60 \end{array}$$

1.
$$\begin{array}{r} 6 \\ \times\ \boxed{} \\ \hline \end{array}$$

2.
$$\begin{array}{r} 6 \\ \times\ \boxed{} \\ \hline \end{array}$$

3.
$$\begin{array}{r} 6 \\ \times\ \boxed{} \\ \hline \end{array}$$

4.
$$\begin{array}{r} 6 \\ \times\ \boxed{} \\ \hline \end{array}$$

5.
$$\begin{array}{r} 6 \\ \times\ \boxed{} \\ \hline \end{array}$$

6.

$$\begin{array}{r} 6 \\ \times\ \boxed{} \\ \hline \end{array}$$

7.
$$\begin{array}{r} 6 \\ \times\ \boxed{} \\ \hline \end{array}$$

8.
$$\begin{array}{r} 6 \\ \times\ \boxed{} \\ \hline \end{array}$$

9.
$$\begin{array}{r} 6 \\ \times\ \boxed{} \\ \hline \end{array}$$

10.

$$\begin{array}{r} 6 \\ \times\ \boxed{} \\ \hline \end{array}$$

Write the answers in order from smallest to greatest.

_____, _____, _____, _____, _____, _____, _____, _____, _____, _____

4 Practice •••••••••••••••••••• Multiplying by 7's

Directions: Solve each problem and write the answer. Color in the answers on the hundreds board below.

1. 7 x 9 = _____ **4.** 7 x 10 = _____ **7.** 7 x 6 = _____ **10.** 7 x 5 = _____

2. 7 x 2 = _____ **5.** 7 x 4 = _____ **8.** 7 x 8 = _____ **11.** 7 x 11 = _____

3. 7 x 7 = _____ **6.** 7 x 3 = _____ **9.** 7 x 1 = _____ **12.** 7 x 12 = _____

1	2	3	4	5	6	7	8	9	10
11	12	13	14	15	16	17	18	19	20
21	22	23	24	25	26	27	28	29	30
31	32	33	34	35	36	37	38	39	40
41	42	43	44	45	46	47	48	49	50
51	52	53	54	55	56	57	58	59	60
61	62	63	64	65	66	67	68	69	70
71	72	73	74	75	76	77	78	79	80
81	82	83	84	85	86	87	88	89	90
91	92	93	94	95	96	97	98	99	100

Directions: Write <, >, or = in the circle to solve each problem. Use the examples as a guide.

5 < 7 **(5 is *less than* 7)**

7 > 5 **(7 is *greater than* 5)**

5 = 5 **(5 *equals* 5)**

13. 7 x 7 ◯ 49 **14.** 6 x 7 ◯ 24 **15.** 3 x 7 ◯ 36 **16.** 9 x 7 ◯ 65

Extension

On the hundreds chart above, extend the pattern all the way to 100 and find out what other numbers are multiples of 7.

Directions: Each of the math problems has a missing factor or product. Cut out the numbers at the bottom of the page. Use the numbers to complete each math problem. (Each number can only be used one time.) After all of the problems have been solved, glue the numbers down.

1.
8
x ☐
———
8 0

2.
8
x 0
———
☐

3.
8
x ☐
———
2 4

4.
8
x ☐
———
4 8

5.
8
x ☐
———
4 0

6.
8
x 8
———
6 ☐

7.
☐
x 1
———
8

8.
8
x ☐
———
5 6

9.
8
x 2
———
☐ 6

10.
8
x ☐
———
7 2

11.
8
x 4
———
3 ☐

12.
8
x ☐
———
8 8

| 0 | 1 | 2 | 3 | 4 | 5 | 6 | 7 | 8 | 9 | 10 | 11 |

Learning Notes

In this unit children will . . .

- learn to multiply by 9's as well as learn the "rule of 9."
- complete a multiplication table for the numbers 0 to 10.
- review basic multiplication skills by playing Six-in-a-Row (similar to Bingo®).

Materials

- counters—beans, pennies, multilink cubes, etc.
- 2 nine-sided dice for each small group of children

Teaching the Lesson

1. "Warm up" the children by counting by 9's to 100 (or more).
2. Go over the "rule of 9" with the children: When multiplying a factor by 9, the digits in the product added together equal 9. Have the children verify this rule by finding the product to the following problems.

   9 x 1 = 9 (9 + 0 = 9)   9 x 12 = 108 (1 + 0 + 8 = 9)   9 x 3 = 27 (2 + 7 = 9)

   9 x 10 = 90 (9 + 0 = 9)   9 x 13 = 117 (1 + 1 + 7 = 9)   9 x 7 = 63 (6 + 3 = 9)

3. Go over the 9's practice sheet (page 22).

Six-in-a-Row

Six-in-a-Row is similar to Bingo and is a great way to review the basic math facts. Make copies of the playing boards (page 23). Have the children write one number in each square. (A list of the numbers to use in the game are listed on page 23.) To play the game, each player rolls the two nine-sided dice and multiplies the two numbers together. Each student uses a counter to cover the product on his or her number board. Other students will use a counter to cover each matching number on their boards. Play continues in the above manner until one player has 6 counters in a row. (*Variation:* Enlarge the playing boards. Have the children write the two factors in the same square as the product.)

9	4	47	7	18	81
11	16	10	44	50	27
72	54	96	25	14	60
26	64	15	2	32	48
75	88	80	62	70	5
24	13	36	96	8	1

Multiplication Table

Model for the children how to fill in the multiplication table (page 24) by multiplying one factor by the other factors (going horizontally or vertically across the paper). For example: 0 x 0 = 0; 0 x 1 = 0; 0 x 2 = 0. As the children complete the table, ask them if they have noticed any pattern to the numbers. Once the table is completed by the children, it can be kept in a math folder and used as a reference tool.

x	0	1	2	3	4	5	6	7	8	9	10
0	0	0	0	0	0	0	0	0	0	0	0
	0 x 0	0 x 1	0 x 2	0 x 3	0 x 4	0 x 5	0 x 6	0 x 7	0 x 8	0 x 9	0 x 10

When multiplying by 9's, the digits in the answer always add to 9.

2 sets with 9 jellybeans in each set or 2 x 9 = 18

If you add the digits in the product (answer), they should equal 9. (1 + 8 = 9)

Directions: Solve each problem. Check each answer. The first one has already been done for you.

1.	2.	3.	4.
9 x 4 ___ **36**	9 x 9 ___	9 x 1 ___	9 x 7 ___

__3__ + __6__ = __9__   ___ + ___ = ___   ___ + ___ = ___   ___ + ___ = ___

5.	6.	7.	8.
9 x 6 ___	9 x 5 ___	9 x 8 ___	9 x 3 ___

___ + ___ = ___   ___ + ___ = ___   ___ + ___ = ___   ___ + ___ = ___

9. What happens when 9 is multiplied by 0? _____

10. What do the following problems all have in common?

3 x 12   2 x 18   6 x 6   9 x 4   36 x 1

_____

5 ▶Practice •••••••••••••• Multiplication by Playing Six-in-a-Row

Directions: Write each one of the following numbers on the playing boards. All numbers must be used—no repeating of numbers is allowed! Take two 9-sided dice and roll them. Multiply the two numbers and use a counter to cover the answer on the playing board. The first player to have six counters in a row (either vertically, horizontally, or diagonally) wins the game!

Numbers to use: 1, 2, 3, 4, 5, 6, 7, 8, 9, 10, 12, 14, 15, 16, 18, 20, 21, 24, 25, 27, 28, 30, 32, 35, 36, 40, 42, 45, 48, 49, 54, 56, 63, 64, 72, 81

Playing Board #1

Playing Board #2

Playing Board #3

Playing Board #4

Directions: Complete the multiplication table by filling in the missing numbers.

X	0	1	2	3	4	5	6	7	8	9	10
0	0										
1		1									
2			4								
3				9							
4					16						
5						25					
6							36				
7								49			
8									64		
9										81	
10											100

1. What did you notice about the chart as you filled in the numbers?

_____

2. What could you do to make sure that the correct numbers were being written in the correct spaces? _____

3. What is the quickest way to count to 100? Why?_____

_____

6 ▶ How to ···· Multiply 2-, 3-, and 4-Digit Numbers Without Regrouping

Learning Notes

In this unit children will . . .

- learn to multiply 2-, 3-, and 4-digit numbers by a single factor without regrouping.
- review place value to 4 places—ones, tens, hundreds, and thousands.

Materials

Ten 3" x 5" (8 cm x 13 cm) index cards cut in half (3" x 2 ½" or 8 cm x 7 cm) for each child or pair of children. (Make 5 sets of cards numbered 0 to 3.)

Teaching the Lesson

1. Use the numbered index cards to model how to multiply 2-, 3-, and 4-digit numbers without regrouping. Shuffle the cards and place in a stack facedown.

Multiplying a 2-Digit Number

Step 1:
Multiply the number in the ones column by 3.

$$3\;\boxed{2}$$
$$x\;\boxed{3}$$
$$\overline{\hphantom{00}6}$$

Step 2:
Multiply the number in the tens column by 3.

$$\boxed{3}\;2$$
$$x\;\boxed{3}$$
$$\overline{96}$$

Multiplying a 3-Digit Number

Step 1:
Multiply the number in the ones column by 3.

$$1\;2\;\boxed{0}$$
$$x\;\boxed{3}$$
$$\overline{\hphantom{0000}0}$$

Step 2:
Multiply the number in the tens column by 3.

$$1\;\boxed{2}\;0$$
$$x\;\boxed{3}$$
$$\overline{\hphantom{00}6\;0}$$

Step 3:
Multiply the number in the hundreds column by 3.

$$\boxed{1}\;2\;0$$
$$x\;\boxed{3}$$
$$\overline{3\;6\;0}$$

Multiplying a 4-Digit Number

Step 1: Multiply the number in the ones column by 2.

$$1\;2\;0\;\boxed{3}$$
$$x\;\boxed{2}$$
$$\overline{\hphantom{0000}6}$$

Step 2: Multiply the number in the tens column by 2.

$$1\;2\;\boxed{0}\;3$$
$$x\;\boxed{2}$$
$$\overline{\hphantom{00}0\;6}$$

Step 3: Multiply the number in the hundreds column by 2.

$$1\;\boxed{2}\;0\;3$$
$$x\;\boxed{2}$$
$$\overline{4\;0\;6}$$

Step 4: Multiply the number in the thousands column by 2.

$$\boxed{1}\;2\;0\;3$$
$$x\;\boxed{2}$$
$$\overline{2,4\;0\;6}$$

2. Have the children practice multiplying 2-, 3-, and 4-digit numbers using the index cards and recording the two factors and the product on a piece of paper.

3. Go over the practice sheets with the children (pages 26–28).

Remember these two steps when multiplying 2-digit numbers.

Step 1: Start with the numbers in the ones column. Multiply 0 x 6 and record the product.	$\begin{array}{r} 1\boxed{0} \\ \times\, \boxed{6} \\ \hline 0 \end{array}$
Step 2: Move to the tens column. Multiply 1 x 6 and record the product.	$\begin{array}{r} \boxed{1}\,0 \\ \times\, \boxed{6} \\ \hline 6\,0 \end{array}$

Directions: Solve each multiplication problem. Use the answers and the letters in each star to decode the secret message.

Secret Message:

Multiplying 3-digit numbers follows the same steps as multiplying 2-digit numbers.

Step 1: Start in the ones column. Multiply 3 x 2. Record the product.

$$\begin{array}{r} 1\ 3\ \boxed{2} \\ \times\ \boxed{3} \\ \hline 6 \end{array}$$

Step 2: Move to the tens column. Multiply 3 x 3 and record the product.

$$\begin{array}{r} 1\ \boxed{3}\ 2 \\ \times\ \boxed{3} \\ \hline 9\ 6 \end{array}$$

Step 3: Move to the hundreds column. Multiply 3 x 1 and record the product.

$$\begin{array}{r} \boxed{1}\ 3\ 2 \\ \times\ \boxed{3} \\ \hline 3\ 9\ 6 \end{array}$$

Directions: Solve each math problem and answer each question.

1.
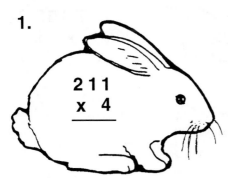

$$\begin{array}{r} 2\ 1\ 1 \\ \times\ 4 \\ \hline \end{array}$$

In the answer what number is in the tens place? _____

2.

$$\begin{array}{r} 3\ 2\ 0 \\ \times\ 3 \\ \hline \end{array}$$

In the answer what number is in the hundreds place? _____

3.
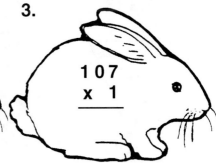

$$\begin{array}{r} 1\ 0\ 7 \\ \times\ 1 \\ \hline \end{array}$$

In the answer what number is in the ones place? _____

4.
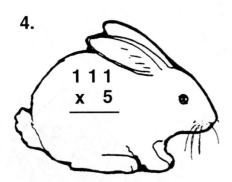

$$\begin{array}{r} 1\ 1\ 1 \\ \times\ 5 \\ \hline \end{array}$$

In the answer what number is in the tens place? _____

5.

$$\begin{array}{r} 8\ 4\ 8 \\ \times\ 1 \\ \hline \end{array}$$

In the answer what number is in the hundreds place? _____

6.

$$\begin{array}{r} 3\ 1\ 3 \\ \times\ 3 \\ \hline \end{array}$$

In the answer what number is in the ones place? _____

When multiplying 4-digit numbers, follow the same steps as multiplying 2-digit numbers.

Step 1: Start in the ones column. Multiply 2 x 3 and record the product.	**Step 2:** Move to the tens column. Multiply 2 x 4 and record the product.	**Step 3:** Move to the hundreds column. Multiply 2 x 3 and record the product.	**Step 4:** Move to the thousands column. Multiply 2 x 2 and record the product. Don't forget to insert a comma to separate the thousands from the hundreds.
2,34**3** x **2** ——— 6	2,3**4**3 x **2** ——— 86	2,**3**43 x **2** ——— 6 86	**2,**343 x **2** ——— 4,686

Directions: Solve the multiplication problems. Then draw a line from a kite to its matching kite ribbon.

1.
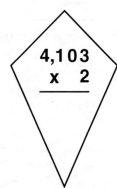

3,333
x   3

8,206

1,261

7.
7,108
x   1

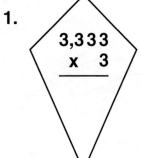
7,108

4,608

8,488

2.
4,103
x   2

6.
2,304
x   2

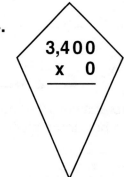
0

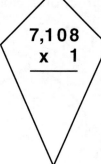
9,999

3.
1,261
x   1

4.
3,400
x   0

5.
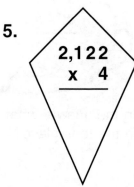
2,122
x   4

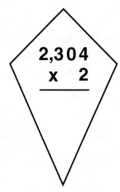
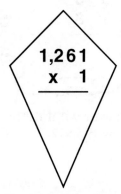

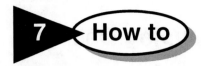

Learning Notes

In this unit children will learn to multiply 2-, 3-, and 4-digit numbers with regrouping one or more times.

Teaching the Lesson

1. Show the children the process of multiplying with regrouping one time.

Step 1: Begin multiplying in the ones column.	Step 2: Move to the tens column and multiply and then add the regrouped number.	Step 3: Move to the hundreds column and multiply.
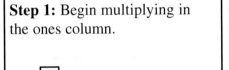	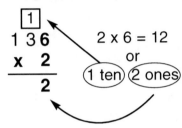	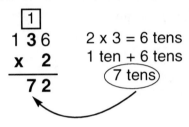

2. Show the children the process of multiplying with regrouping more than one time.

Step 1: Begin multiplying in the ones column. Regroup if necessary.	Step 2: Move to the tens column and multiply. Then add the regrouped number.	Step 3: Move to the hundreds column and multiply. Then add the regrouped number.
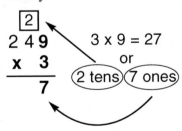	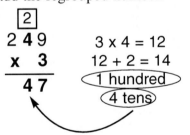	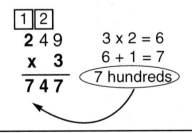

3. Have the children practice multiplying different factors and regrouping one, two, or three times.

4. Go over the practice sheets with the children (pages 30–32).

Step 1: Multiply the factors in the ones column (4 x 6 = 24 or 2 tens and 4 ones). Record the 4 ones in the ones column and regroup the 2 tens to the tens column.	**Step 2:** Move to the tens column. Multiply the factors 6 x 0 and add the 2 tens (6 x 0 = 0 + 2 = 2 tens). Record the 2 tens.	**Step 3:** Move to the hundreds column. Multiply 6 x 1 and record the answer.
$\boxed{2}$ 1 0 4 x 6 = 24 —— 4	$\boxed{2}$ 1 0 4 x 6 —— 2 4	$\boxed{2}$ 1 0 4 x 6 —— 6 2 4

Directions: Solve each multiplication problem.

1. $\square$
$$106$$
$$\times\ 8$$

2. $\square$
$$108$$
$$\times\ 7$$

3. $\square$
$$29$$
$$\times\ 2$$

4. $\square$
$$1,114$$
$$\times\ 7$$

5. $\square$
$$102$$
$$\times\ 9$$

6. $\square$
$$2,328$$
$$\times\ \ \ 3$$

7. $\square$
$$107$$
$$\times\ 9$$

8. $\square$
$$15$$
$$\times\ 2$$

Directions: Complete each of the math problems.

9. $3 \times 9 + 5 =$ _____

10. $5 \times 9 - 15 =$ _____

11. $4 \times 10 + 25 =$ _____

12. $6 \times 6 - 24 =$ _____

13. $1 \times 0 + 0 =$ _____

14. $2 \times 8 - 13 =$ _____

15. $20 \times 2 + 50 - 60 =$ _____

16. $25 \times 3 - 40 + 15 =$ _____

When multiplying factors which involve regrouping more than one time, remember these three steps.

Step 1: Start in the ones column. Multiply the factors 2 x 8 (2 x 8 = 16 or 1 ten and 6 ones). Record the 6 ones in the ones column and regroup the 1 ten to the tens column.	**Step 2:** Move to the tens column. Multiply 2 x 9. 2 x 9 = 18 + the ten that was regrouped = 19 tens or 1 hundred and 9 tens. Record the 9 tens in the tens column and regroup the 1 hundred to the hundreds column.	**Step 3:** Move to the hundreds column. Multiply 2 x 1 and add the 1 hundred that was regrouped (2 x 1 = 2 + 1 = 3 hundreds). Record the number in the hundreds column.
[1] 1 9 8 x 2 = 16 6	[1][1] 1 9 8 x 2 9 6	[1][1] 1 9 8 x 2 3 9 6

Directions: Solve each multiplication problem.

1. 138
    x 3

2. 116
    x 7

3. 125
    x 9

4. 1,027
    x 7

5. 173
    x 4

6. 166
    x 6

7. 1,238
    x 3

8. 164
    x 7

9. 1,053
    x 6

10. 235
    x 4

11. 159
    x 6

12. 245
    x 4

Directions: Take fifty 3" x 5" (8 cm x 13 cm) index cards and make five sets of cards numbered 0 to 9.

Shuffle the cards and place in a stack facedown. Turn over the top five cards and lay them out in order. Multiply the top factor by the bottom factor.

$$
\begin{array}{ccccc}
 & 2 & 6 & 3 & \\
\boxed{8} & , & \boxed{3} & \boxed{9} & \boxed{5} \\
 & & & & \boxed{7} \\
\hline
5 & 8 & , & 7 & 6 & 5
\end{array}
$$

1. □ , □ □ □
   X □

2. □ , □ □ □
   X □

3. □ , □ □ □
   X □

4. □ , □ □ □
   X □

5. □ , □ □ □
   X □

6. □ , □ □ □
   X □

7. □ , □ □ □
   X □

8. □ , □ □ □
   X □

9. □ , □ □ □
   X □

10. □ , □ □ □
    X □

11. □ , □ □ □
    X □

12. □ , □ □ □
    X □

How to •••• Use Multiplication in Different Ways

Learning Notes

In this unit children will . . .

- learn to find the volume for different sizes of cubes.
- round factors to the nearest hundreds and multiply to find the estimated product.
- learn to multiply factors with decimal points.

Materials

- "cubes" found in or near the children's desks—pencil boxes, books, etc.
- ruler

Teaching the Lesson

- **Finding the Volume**

  Go over the formula for volume (V = l x w x h or Volume = length x width x height) with the children.

  Have the children find objects in or near their desks that are cube shaped. Have the children measure the length, width, and height of each object.

  Model how to figure out the volume for the different sizes of cubes.

- **Estimating Products**

  Review the concept of rounding to the nearest hundred with the children. Remind them that if the number in the tens place is 0, 1, 2, 3, or 4, round down. If the number in the tens place is 5, 6, 7, 8, or 9, round up.

  Verbally, give the children different numbers and have them round the number to the nearest hundreds.

  Examples: 319 (300), 625 (600), 457 (500), 198 (200)

- **Multiplying Decimals**

  When multiplying a whole number times a decimal, the children do the multiplying in the same process used when multiplying numbers without decimals. Multiplication always begins at the first number on the right and moves to the last number on the left. After finding the product, the children need to look at the place of the decimal point in the factor. If the decimal point is two places to the left, then place the decimal point two places to the left in the product.

Sample A	Sample B
⁴ $ 0.18 x 6 ――― $1.08 The decimal is two places to the left.	² $ 1.26 x 4 ――― $5.04 The decimal is two places to the left.

The number of small cubes that will fit into a large cube (box) is the volume. To find the volume of a cube, multiply the length times the width times the height.
The formula looks like this: **V = l x w x h**

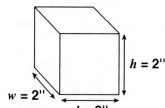

$h = 2''$
$w = 2''$
$l = 2''$

V = 2" x 2" x 2"

V = 4" x 2"

V = 8 cubic inches

Directions: Find the volume for each shape.

1.

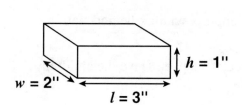

$w = 2''$
$l = 3''$
$h = 1''$

___ **X** ___ **X** ___ = ___
  l   w   h

The volume is
____ cubic inches.

2.

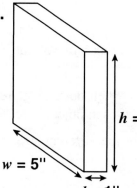

$h = 5''$
$w = 5''$
$l = 1''$

___ **X** ___ **X** ___ = ___
  l   w   h

The volume is
____ cubic inches.

3.

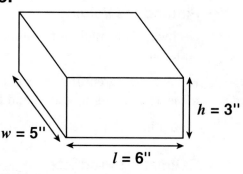

$h = 3''$
$w = 5''$
$l = 6''$

___ **X** ___ **X** ___ = ___
  l   w   h

The volume is
____ cubic inches.

4.

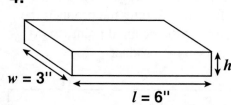

$w = 3''$
$l = 6''$
$h = 1''$

___ **X** ___ **X** ___ = ___
  l   w   h

The volume is
____ cubic inches.

5.

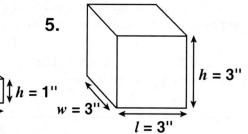

$h = 3''$
$w = 3''$
$l = 3''$

___ **X** ___ **X** ___ = ___
  l   w   h

The volume is
____ cubic inches.

6.

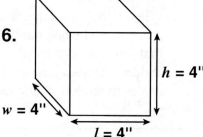

$h = 4''$
$w = 4''$
$l = 4''$

___ **X** ___ **X** ___ = ___
  l   w   h

The volume is
____ cubic inches.

Estimate the product by rounding the factor to the nearest hundred and then multiplying by the other factor.

Example

Step 1: Read the word problem.
Jerry has 121 trading cards in each box. Jerry has 6 boxes in all.

Step 2: Round the factor to the nearest 100.
The number 121 is rounded down to 100.

Step 3: Multiply the two factors to arrive at the estimated product (100 x 6 = 600).
Jerry has about 600 trading cards.

Remember: If the number in the tens place is 0, 1, 2, 3, or 4, round down. If the number in the tens place is 5, 6, 7, 8, or 9, round up.

Directions: Read each word problem. Round the factor to the nearest hundred and multiply to find the estimated product.

1. Each apple tree has 321 apples. About how many apples are there on 4 trees?

    _____ is rounded to _____.

    _____ x _____ = _____

    There are about _____ apples on 4 trees.

2. One grasshopper lays 149 eggs. About how many eggs do 6 grasshoppers lay?

    _____ is rounded to _____.

    _____ x _____ = _____

    Six grasshoppers can lay about _____ eggs.

3. There are 110 marbles in a bag. About how many marbles in 9 bags?

    _____ is rounded to _____.

    _____ x _____ = _____

    There are about _____ marbles in 9 bags.

4. There are 360 buttons in a box. About how many buttons in 4 boxes?

    _____ is rounded to _____.

    _____ x _____ = _____

    There are about _____ buttons in 4 boxes.

5. A sunflower has 451 seeds. About how many seeds are on 2 sunflowers?

    _____ is rounded to _____.

    _____ x _____ = _____

    There are about _____ seeds on 2 sunflowers.

6. One group of ladybugs has 269 spots. About how many spots on 2 groups of ladybugs?

    _____ is rounded to _____.

    _____ x _____ = _____

    There are about _____ spots on 2 groups of ladybugs.

When multiplying a whole number times a decimal, start with the last number on the right (6 x 5 = 30 or 3 tenths and 0 hundredths). Record the 0 in the hundredths column and regroup the 3 tenths to the tenths column.

	ones	tenths	hundredths
$	0	.1³	5
x			6
			0

Move to the tenths column. Multiply 6 x 1 and then add the 3 tenths that were regrouped. Record the 9 in the tenths column.

	ones	tenths	hundredths
$	0	.1³	5
x			6
		9	0

Finally, multiply 6 x 0 and record the 0 in the ones column. In the factor $0.15, the decimal place is two places to the left of the last number (5). In the product (answer), write the decimal point two places to the left of the last number and add a dollar sign.

	ones	tenths	hundredths
$	0	.1³	5
x			6
$	0	.9	0

Directions: Solve each problem. Remember to include the dollar sign and the decimal point in each answer.

1.
$0.25
x 3

2.
$0.95
x 2

3.
$0.36
x 4

4.
$0.46
x 9

5.
$0.17
x 6

6.
$0.81
x 7

7.
$2.11
x 3

8.
$0.13
x 8

9.
$1.05
x 5

10.
$0.75
x 2

11.
$0.60
x 9

12.
$3.54
x 4

Use Graphs and Order of Operation in Multiplication Problems

Learning Notes

In this unit children will . . .

- use information from a graph to write multiplication problems.
- use the "order of operation" in solving math problems.
- read word problems and write math sentences using both multiplication and addition and/or subtraction.

Materials

Make a chart showing the order of operation.

> ### Order of Operation
>
> 1. Do the operation in parentheses first.
>
> 2. Multiply in order going from left to right.
>
> 3. Add and/or subtract in order going from left to right.

Teaching the Lesson

- ### Using Graphs to Multiply

  Go over the graph with the children. Point out the legend. The legend tells the children that each animal in the graph represents 7 animals.

  Ask the children:

  > "How many bats does 1 bat on the graph represent?" *(7)*
  >
  > "How many possums do 3 possums on the graph represent? *(7 x 3 = 21)*

  Have the children complete the practice sheet.

- ### Order of Operation in Multiplication Problems

  On the chalkboard, write a problem using both multiplication and/or addition and subtraction. For example, (3 + 7) x 8 = ? *Ask:* "What part of the problem should be done first?" (*the operation in parentheses*) As a class solve the problem. *(10 x 8 = 80)*

  Give the children several more problems so that they feel comfortable working with the order of operations. Have the children complete the practice sheet.

- ### Multiplication Word Problems

  Model how to read the word problems and write the math sentences that tell about the word problem. Have the children complete the practice sheet.

Directions: Use the picture graph below to answer the questions.

Remember, to show your work for each problem and that each animal picture stands for 7 animals.

How many of each animal are there in all?

Legend

= 7

Each animal picture represents 7 animals.

bat	🦇	🦇	🦇	🦇	🦇			
owl	🦉	🦉	🦉	🦉	🦉	🦉	🦉	
cat	🐱	🐱	🐱					
skunk	🦨	🦨	🦨	🦨	🦨	🦨		
dog	🐶	🐶	🐶	🐶	🐶	🐶	🐶	🐶

1. ☐
   x ☐
   _____

There are _____ bats in all.

2. ☐
   x ☐
   _____

There are _____ owls in all.

3. ☐
   x ☐
   _____

There are _____ cats in all.

4. ☐
   x ☐
   _____

There are _____ skunks in all.

5. ☐
   x ☐
   _____

There are _____ dogs in all.

6. How many animals are there in all?

There are _____ animals in all.

When a math problem has more than one operation—multiplying, dividing, adding, and/or subtracting—in one problem, solve the math problem in the following order.

- **Step 1:** Do the operation in parentheses first.

- **Step 2:** Multiply and/or divide in order going from left to right.

- **Step 3:** Add and/or subtract in order going from left to right.

Directions: Find out what your answer is for each problem. The first one has already been done for you. Remember to show your work.

1. $(25 \times 3) + 17 - 39 = ?$

     $75 + 17 = 92 - 39 = 53$

My answer is _____**53**_____.

2. $(15 \times 6) - 42 + 21 = ?$

My answer is _____.

3. $(19 \times 4) - 54 + 0 = ?$

My answer is _____.

4. $(63 \times 2) - 80 + 1 = ?$

My answer is _____.

5. $(37 \times 7) - 100 + 49 = ?$

My answer is _____.

6. $(35 \times 5) + 15 - 10 = ?$

My answer is _____.

Directions: Read and solve each word problem. The first one has already been done for you. Remember to show your work.

1. There are 5 holes with 6 skunks in each hole. 9 of the skunks climbed out of the holes. How many skunks are still in the holes?

$$5 \times 6 = 30$$
$$30 - 9 = 21$$

There are __21__ skunks in the holes.

2. One wolf eats 9 bones each day. How many bones would 6 wolves eat in one week?

The 6 wolves would eat _____ bones in one week.

3. There are 7 trees with 3 possums in each tree. 6 possums climbed down. How many possums are still in the trees?

There are _____ possums in the trees.

4. There are 4 trees with 8 owls in each tree. 9 more owls came and joined them. How many owls are now in the trees?

There are _____ owls in the trees.

One bat can catch 7 mosquitoes each night. How many mosquitoes can 2 bats catch in one night? in one week (7 days)? in one month (30 days)? and in one year (365 days)?

5. In one night, two bats can catch _____ mosquitoes.

6. In one week, two bats can catch _____ mosquitoes.

7. In one month, two bats can catch _____ mosquitoes.

8. In one year, two bats can catch _____ mosquitoes.

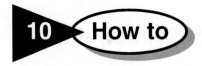

Use Multiplication in Brain Teasers, Problem Solving, and Technology

Learning Notes

In this unit children will . . .

- figure out the "rule" by looking for multiplication patterns within given sets of numbers.
- decode a secret message by multiplying the two factors and writing the number word for the product.
- multiply two factors and graph the product.
- make conclusions based upon the information shown on the graph.
- use their multiplication skills to solve word problems.
- go on the Internet to review and practice multiplication skills.

Materials

Each child or pair of children will need twenty-six 3" x 5" (8 cm x 13 cm) index cards cut in half (3" x 2 ½" or 8 cm x 7 cm). Make four sets of cards numbered 0–12.

Teaching the Lesson

Uncover the Multiplication Pattern

The children will look at sets of numbers and figure out the multiplication rule. The children can test the rule by filling in the missing factor or product. The rule must fit all of the numbers in the set.

Multiply to Decipher the Hidden Message

The children will review basic multiplication skills. Instead of using numerals to record the product, the children will write the number word—one letter on each line. After solving all of the problems, the letters in the circles will spell out a secret message.

Graph It!

Have the children shuffle the index cards and place them in a stack facedown. The children will turn over the top two cards and multiply the factors. The children will record the factors and the product in the appropriate spaces. After one column is completely filled, have the children look at the graph and write two to three sentences about their results.

Using Multiplication at the Candy Shop

The children will read the word problems and obtain the prices for each candy listed in the word problem. The children will solve the word problem and write a sentence about the answer.

Math Games on the Internet

The children will go to the Fun Brain Web site and play multiplication baseball. The children can select the level of difficulty for the multiplication problems.

Directions: Solve each pattern by multiplying by a certain number. Write the rule for the pattern. The first one is done for you as an example.

1.

In	Out
4	28
5	35
9	63
3	21
8	56
1	7

The rule is to multiply by 7.

2.

In	Out
2	4
3	6
___	18
6	___
4	___
7	14
8	___

The rule is _____.

3.

In	Out
3	9
___	12
2	___
___	18
9	___
8	___
1	___

The rule is _____.

4.

In	Out
5	30
___	42
4	___
3	___
___	6
0	___
9	___

The rule is _____.

5.

In	Out
6	54
3	___
7	63
___	36
5	___
___	0
9	___

The rule is _____.

6.

In	Out
5	25
___	15
8	___
1	___
___	45
0	___
___	30

The rule is _____.

7.

In	Out
2	2
8	___
___	7
___	3
9	___
5	___
4	___

The rule is _____.

8.

In	Out
4	___
___	4
___	20
9	36
3	___
6	24
___	28

The rule is _____.

9.

In	Out
___	16
3	___
6	48
___	40
___	8
9	72
4	___

The rule is _____.

Directions: Solve each math problem and then write each letter in the number word answer on the lines. After solving all of the problems, read the letters in the circles going from top to bottom to discover the message. The first one is done for you.

(M)

1. 2 x 2   F   O (U) R
‗   ‗ ‗   ‗

2. 3 x 4   ‗ ‗ ‗ (○) ‗ ‗

3. 1 x 10   (○) ‗ ‗

4. 1 x 6   ‗ (○) ‗

(P)

5. 11 x 1   ‗ (○) ‗ ‗ ‗ ‗

6. 5 x 5   ‗ ‗ ‗ ‗ ‗ (○) ‗ ‗ ‗

7. 30 x 3   ‗ (○) ‗ ‗ ‗

8. 3 x 9   ‗ ‗ ‗ (○) ‗ ‗ ‗ ‗ ‗ ‗

9. 9 x 9   ‗ ‗ (○) ‗ ‗ ‗ ‗ ‗ ‗

10. 8 x 7   ‗ (○) ‗ ‗ ‗ ‗ ‗

11. 15 x 4   (○) ‗ ‗ ‗ ‗

12. 7 x 7   (○) ‗ ‗ ‗ ‗ ‗ ‗ ‗ ‗

13. 7 x 2   ‗ ‗ (○) ‗ ‗ ‗ ‗

14. 9 x 8   ‗ ‗ ‗ ‗ (○) ‗ ‗ ‗ ‗

Directions

1. Cut twenty-six 3" x 5" (8 cm x 13 cm) index cards in half (3" x 2 ½" or 8 cm x 7 cm). Make four sets of cards numbered 0–12.

2. Shuffle the cards and place them in a stack facedown.

3. Turn over the top two cards and multiply them.

4. In the correct column, record the two factors and the product in the box. (Make sure to start in the first available space above the column heading.)

5. Repeat the above steps until one column is completely filled.

Index Cards	**9**	**6**

9 x 6 = 54

		9 x 6 = 54	
0–20	21–40	41–60	61–80

0–20	**21–40**	**41–60**	**61–80**	**81–100**	**101–120**	**121–140**	**141–160**

Write two to three sentences about your graph.

_____

_____

_____

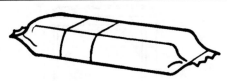

jumbo candy bar
$1.18

licorice
$0.27 a piece

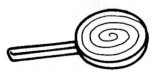

big lollipop
$2.27

big cookie
$1.65

jellybeans
$0.89 a pound

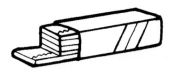

pack of gum
$0.39

Directions: Read and solve each word problem. The first one has already been done for you. Remember to show your work.

1. James has $4.50 to spend at the candy shop. Does James have enough money to buy 2 jumbo candy bars and 3 pieces of licorice?

(2 x $1.18) + (3 x $0.27) =
$2.36 + $0.81 = $3.17

Yes, James has enough to buy the candy.

_____

2. Cedric buys 5 pounds of jellybeans. How much money did Cedric spend?

3. Rachel has $10.00 to spend. She buys 4 big cookies and 1 big lollipop. How much money does Rachel have left?

4. Salvador buys 6 packs of gum and 2 big lollipops. How much money did Salvador spend?

12 ▷ Technology •••••••••• Math Games on the Internet

There are exciting math games that can be found on the Internet.

Directions

1. Type in *http://www.funbrain.com*

2. Click on *Math Baseball*

3. Click on *Multiplication* and pick the level—easy or hard.

4. Play ball!

Directions: Answer the following questions.

1. What level of math problems did you choose? _____

_____

_____

2. Did you play the game by yourself or with a partner? _____

_____

_____

3. What was the score at the end of the game? _____

_____

_____

_____

4. What did you like about the game? _____

_____

_____

5. Would you play this game again? Why or why not? _____

_____

_____

_____

Page 6
1. 5
2. 10
3. 3
4. 6
5. 4
6. 8
7. 1
8. 2
9. 7
10. 14
11. 6
12. 12
13. 6, 8, 10, 12, 14, 16, 18, 20, 22, 24
14. 12, 16, 20, 24, 28, 32, 36, 40, 44, 48
15. 15, 20, 25, 30, 35, 40, 45, 50, 55, 60
16. 18, 24, 30, 36, 42, 48, 54, 60, 66, 72

Page 7
1. 2 + 2 + 2 + 2 = 8
2. 4 x 2 = 8
3. 5 + 5 = 10
4. 2 x 5 = 10
5. 4 + 4 + 4 = 12
6. 3 x 4 = 12
7. 6 + 6 = 12
8. 2 x 6 = 12
9. 1 + 1 + 1 + 1 + 1 + 1 = 6
10. 6 x 1 = 6
11. 3 + 3 + 3 + 3 = 12
12. 4 x 3 = 12

Page 8
1. 6
2. 10
3. 2
4. 4
5. 8
6. 14
7. 12
8. 18

Page 10
chart: 2, 4, 6, 8, 10, 12, 14, 16, 18, 20
1. 2
2. 18
3. 12
4. 14
5. 8
6. 20
7. 4
8. 0
9. 6

Page 11
Count by 3's: 0, 3, 6, 9, 12, 15, 18, (21), 24, 27, 30
1. G. 3
2. A. 27
3. D. 21
4. E. 12
5. I. 30
6. B. 15
7. H. 24
8. F. 9
9. C. 18

Page 12
1. 2
2. 1
3. 2
4. 4
5. 10
6. 2
7. 14
8. 8
9. 2
10. 20
11. 1
12. 6
13. 3
14. 12
15. 5
16. 3
17. 21
18. 8
19. 2 x 6 = 12
 Joanie has 12 marbles in all.
20. 8 x 2 = 16
 The 8 baskets will hold 16 apples in all.
21. 3 x 9 = 27
 There are 27 spider eggs in all.
22. 3 x 5 = 15
 Mary's dogs eat 15 dog biscuits a day.
23. 3 x 10 = 30
 Katie reads 30 pages a day.
24. 15 x 2 = 30
 Sasha needs to buy 30 cupcakes.

Page 14
Problems 1–12: The answers are all 0.
13. 3
14. 9
15. 3
16. 8
17. 5
18. 4
19. 10
20. 9

21. 8
22. 4
23. 2
24. 10

Page 15
(The children are to solve each problem horizontally and then rewrite the problem vertically and solve. The answers are the same for both the horizontal and vertical problems.)
1. 4 x 3 = 12
2. 4 x 7 = 28
3. 4 x 9 = 36
4. 4 x 4 = 16
5. 4 x 2 = 8
6. 4 x 8 = 32

Page 16
1. 10
2. 5
3. 30
4. 55
5. 35
6. 50
7. 25
8. 50
9. 20
10. 45
11. 15
12. 40
13. 20
14. 55

Question: Can you multiply?

Page 18
Answers will vary.

Page 19
1. 63   9. 7
2. 14   10. 35
3. 49   11. 77
4. 70   12. 84
5. 28   13. =
6. 21   14. >
7. 42   15. <
8. 56   16. <

Page 20
1. 10   7. 8
2. 0   8. 7
3. 3   9. 1
4. 6   10. 9
5. 5   11. 2
6. 4   12. 11

Page 22
1. 36; 3 + 6 = 9
2. 81; 8 + 1 = 9
3. 9; 9 + 0 = 9
4. 63; 6 + 3 = 9
5. 54; 5 + 4 = 9
6. 45; 4 + 5 = 9
7. 72; 7 + 2 = 9
8. 27; 2 + 7 = 9

9. The answer is 0.
10. They all have 36 as the product.

Page 24
Problems 1–3: Answers will vary.

X	0	1	2	3	4	5	6	7	8	9	10
0	0	0	0	0	0	0	0	0	0	0	0
1	0	1	2	3	4	5	6	7	8	9	10
2	0	2	4	6	8	10	12	14	16	18	20
3	0	3	6	9	12	15	18	21	24	27	30
4	0	4	8	12	16	20	24	28	32	36	40
5	0	5	10	15	20	25	30	35	40	45	50
6	0	6	12	18	24	30	36	42	48	54	60
7	0	7	14	21	28	35	42	49	56	63	70
8	0	8	16	24	32	40	48	56	64	72	80
9	0	9	18	27	36	45	54	63	72	81	90
10	0	10	20	30	40	50	60	70	80	90	100

Page 26
I. 48   H. 24
T. 73   L. 0
A. 66   R. 36
S. 99   E. 57
S. 44   K. 90
I. 23   E. 82
A. 15   N. 88

Message: Shine like a star!

Page 27
1. 844; tens place: 4
2. 960; hundreds place: 9
3. 107; ones place: 7
4. 555; tens place: 5
5. 848; hundreds place: 8
6. 939; ones place: 9

Page 28
1. 9,999
2. 8,206
3. 1,261
4. 0
5. 8,488
6. 4,608
7. 7,108

Page 30
1. 848   9. 32
2. 756   10. 30
3. 58   11. 65
4. 7,798 12. 12
5. 918   13. 0
6. 6,984 14. 3
7. 963   15. 30
8. 30   16. 50

Page 31
1. 414   7. 3,714
2. 812   8. 1,148
3. 1,125 9. 6,318
4. 7,189 10. 940
5. 692   11. 954
6. 996   12. 980

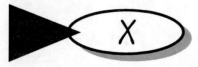

Page 32

Answers will vary.

Page 34

1. 3" x 2" x 1" = 6"
   The volume is 6 cubic inches.
2. 1" x 5" x 5" = 25"
   The volume is 25 cubic inches.
3. 6"x 5" x 3" = 90"
   The volume is 90 cubic inches.
4. 6" x 3" x 1" = 18"
   The volume is 18 cubic inches.
5. 3" x 3" x 3" = 27"
   The volume is 27 cubic inches.
6. 4" x 4" x 4" = 64"
   The volume is 64 cubic inches.

Page 35

1. 321 is rounded to 300.
   4 x 300 = 1,200
   There are about 1,200 apples on 4 trees.
2. 149 is rounded to 100.
   6 x 100 = 600
   6 grasshoppers can lay about 600 eggs.
3. 110 is rounded to 100.
   9 x 100 = 900
   There are about 900 marbles in 9 bags.
4. 360 is rounded to 400.
   4 x 400 = 1,600
   There are about 1,600 buttons in 4 boxes.
5. 451 is rounded to 500.
   2 x 500 = 1,000
   There are about 1,000 seeds on 2 sunflowers.
6. 269 is rounded to 300.
   2 x 300 = 600
   There are about 600 spots on 2 groups of ladybugs.

Page 36

1.	$0.75	7.	$6.33
2.	$1.90	8.	$1.04
3.	$1.44	9.	$5.25
4.	$4.14	10.	$1.50
5.	$1.02	11.	$5.40
6.	$5.67	12.	$14.16

Page 38

1. 5 x 7 = 35
   There are 35 bats in all.
2. 7 x 7 = 49
   There are 49 owls in all.
3. 3 x 7 = 21
   There are 21 cats in all.
4. 6 x 7 = 42
   There are 42 skunks in all.
5. 8 x 7 = 56
   There are 56 dogs in all.
6. 35 + 49 + 21 + 42 + 56
   = 203 animals in all. Or
   5 (bats) + 7 (owls) + 3 (cats) + 6 (skunks) + 8 (dogs) = 29 animals; 29 (animals) x 7 = 203 animals in all

Page 39

1. 75 + 17 = 92 – 39 = 53
   My answer is 53.
2. 90 – 42 = 48 + 21 = 69
   My answer is 69.
3. 76 – 54 = 22 + 0 = 22
   My answer is 22.
4. 126 – 80 = 46 + 1 = 47
   My answer is 47.
5. 259 – 100 = 159 + 49 = 208
   My answer is 208.
6. 175 + 15 = 190 – 10 = 180 My answer is 180.

Page 40

1. 5 x 6 = 30 – 9 = 21
   There are 21 skunks in the holes.
2. 6 x 9 = 54 x 7 = 378
   The 6 wolves would eat 378 bones in one week.
3. 7 x 3 = 21 – 6 = 15
   There are 15 possums in the trees.
4. 4 x 8 = 32 + 9 = 41
   There are 41 owls in the trees.
5. In one night: 14 mosquitoes (2 x 7 = 14)
6. In one week: 98 mosquitoes (14 x 7 = 98)
7. In one month: 420 mosquitoes (14 x 30 = 420)
8. In one year: 5,110 mosquitoes (14 x 365 = 5,110)

Page 42

1. | In | Out |
   |---|---|
   | 4 | 28 |
   | 5 | 35 |
   | 9 | 63 |
   | 3 | 21 |
   | 8 | 56 |
   | 1 | 7 |

   Multiply by 7.

2. | In | Out |
   |---|---|
   | 2 | 4 |
   | 3 | 6 |
   | 9 | 18 |
   | 6 | 12 |
   | 4 | 8 |
   | 7 | 14 |
   | 8 | 16 |

   Multiply by 2.

3. | In | Out |
   |---|---|
   | 3 | 9 |
   | 4 | 12 |
   | 2 | 6 |
   | 6 | 18 |
   | 9 | 27 |
   | 8 | 24 |
   | 1 | 3 |

   Multiply by 3.

4. | In | Out |
   |---|---|
   | 5 | 30 |
   | 7 | 42 |
   | 4 | 24 |
   | 3 | 18 |
   | 1 | 6 |
   | 0 | 0 |
   | 9 | 54 |

   Multiply by 6.

5. | In | Out |
   |---|---|
   | 6 | 54 |
   | 3 | 27 |
   | 7 | 63 |
   | 4 | 36 |
   | 5 | 45 |
   | 0 | 0 |
   | 9 | 81 |

   Multiply by 9.

6. | In | Out |
   |---|---|
   | 5 | 25 |
   | 3 | 15 |
   | 8 | 40 |
   | 1 | 5 |
   | 9 | 45 |
   | 0 | 0 |
   | 6 | 30 |

   Multiply by 5.

7. | In | Out |
   |---|---|
   | 2 | 2 |
   | 8 | 8 |
   | 7 | 7 |
   | 3 | 3 |
   | 9 | 9 |
   | 5 | 5 |
   | 4 | 4 |

   Multiply by 1.

8. | In | Out |
   |---|---|
   | 4 | 16 |
   | 1 | 4 |
   | 5 | 20 |
   | 9 | 36 |
   | 3 | 12 |
   | 6 | 24 |
   | 7 | 28 |

   Multiply by 4.

9. | In | Out |
   |---|---|
   | 2 | 16 |
   | 3 | 24 |
   | 6 | 48 |
   | 5 | 40 |
   | 1 | 8 |
   | 9 | 72 |
   | 4 | 32 |

   Multiply by 8.

Page 43

1. four
2. twelve
3. ten
4. six
5. eleven
6. twenty-five
7. ninety
8. twenty-seven
9. eighty-one
10. fifty-six
11. sixty
12. forty-nine
13. fourteen
14. seventy-two

Message: Multiplying is fun!

Page 44

Graphs and sentences will vary.

Page 45

1. (2 x $1.18) + (3 x $0.27) = $2.36 + $0.81 = $3.17
   Yes, James has enough money to buy the candy.
2. 5 x $0.89 = $4.45
   Cedric spent $4.45
3. (4 x $1.65) + (1 x $2.27) = $6.60 + $2.27 = $8.87
   $10.00 – $8.87 = $1.13
   Rachel has $1.13 left.
4. (6 x $0.39) + (2 x $2.27) = $2.34 + $4.54 = $6.88
   Salvador spent $6.88.

Page 46

Answers will vary.